Little
Pebble™

Baby Animals and Their Homes

BABY ANIMALS In DENS

by Martha E. H. Rustad

raintree
a Capstone company — publishers for children

Raintree is an imprint of Capstone Global Library Limited, a company incorporated in England and Wales having its registered office at 264 Banbury Road, Oxford, OX2 7DY – Registered company number: 6695582

www.raintree.co.uk
myorders@raintree.co.uk

Text © Capstone Global Library Limited 2017
The moral rights of the proprietor have been asserted.

Editorial Credits
Carrie Braulick Sheely, editor; Juliette Peters, designer;
Tracey Engel, media researcher; Katy LaVigne, production specialist

ISBN 978 1 4747 3330 4 (hardback)
20 19 18 17 16
10 9 8 7 6 5 4 3 2 1

British Library Cataloguing in Publication Data
A full catalogue record for this book is available from the British Library.

Acknowledgements
We would like to thank the following for permission to reproduce photographs: Alamy: Rick & Nora Bowers, 8–9, WILDLIFE GmbH, 21; Getty Images: D. Robert & Lorri Franz, 4–5, Thorsten Milse/robertharding, 13; National Geographic Creative: DES & JEN BARTLETT, 17; Newscom: Dave Watts/NHPA/Photoshot, 6–7; NHPA: Photoshot/Gerard Lacz, Front Cover; Shutterstock: Ales Liska, Back Cover and Interior Design Element, Brad Sauter, 1 Bottom Left, David Rasmus, 11, Geoffrey Kuchera, 19, sittipong, Back Cover Design Element, Tony Moran, 3 Bottom Left; Visuals Unlimited: Steve Maslowski, 15

Every effort has been made to contact copyright holders of material reproduced in this book. Any omissions will be rectified in subsequent printings if notice is given to the publisher.

Dig!

A coyote digs a den.

She has cubs.

They stay warm.

Contents

Dens high and low

Some baby animals grow up in dens. Dens hide them from other animals.

Ocelot kittens have
dark spots.
They stay close to mum.
Purr!

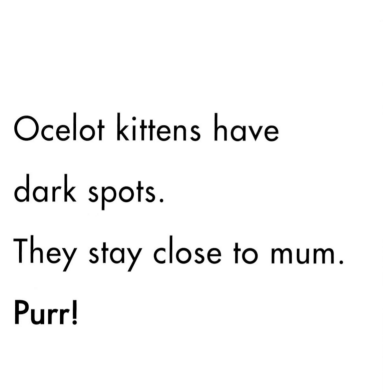

Two bear cubs share a den.

It is in a cave.

They drink milk from mum.

A polar bear den
is in snow.

Cubs peek out.

This den is in a tree.

New raccoon babies

can't see.

Mum keeps them safe.

Growing up

Beaver kits live in dens.

The opening is underwater.

They swim out.

Splash!

Older fox cubs go out.

Sniff! They hunt for mice.

A red panda picks up
her cub.

She finds a new den.

Dens make good homes.

Glossary

cub the young of coyotes, foxes, bears, pandas and some other animals

den a home for some animals; a den may be in a cave, hollow log or other sheltered place

hunt to find and kill animals for food

kit the young of beavers, raccoons and some other animals

ocelot a wildcat that lives mainly in Central and South America

Read more

Bears (Froglets Learners), Annabelle Lynch (Franklin Watts, 2015)

Fox (City Safari), Isabel Thomas (Raintree, 2015)

Inside Beaver Lodges (Inside Animal Homes), Emily Wilson (PowerKids Press, 2016)

Websites

www.bbc.co.uk/nature/life/Polar_bear
Learn more about how polar bears live, and view videos of polar bears.

www.animalcorner.co.uk/animals/red-fox/
Learn about the appearance, diet, life cycle and range of red foxes.

Comprehension questions

1. Look at the picture on page 9. Why do you think the kittens have darker spots than the mother? How can this colouring help the kittens stay safe?

2. Red pandas move their cubs to new dens often. Why do you think they do this?

Index